PEB PAPERS

Making better use of school buildings

ORGANISATION FOR ECONOMIC CO-OPERATION AND DEVELOPMENT

ORGANISATION FOR ECONOMIC CO-OPERATION AND DEVELOPMENT

Pursuant to Article 1 of the Convention signed in Paris on 14th December 1960, and which came into force on 30th September 1961, the Organisation for Economic Co-operation and Development (OECD) shall promote policies designed:

- to achieve the highest sustainable economic growth and employment and a rising standard of living in Member countries, while maintaining financial stability, and thus to contribute to the development of the world economy;
- to contribute to sound economic expansion in Member as well as non-member countries in the process of economic development; and
- to contribute to the expansion of world trade on a multilateral, non-discriminatory basis in accordance with international obligations.

The original Member countries of the OECD are Austria, Belgium, Canada, Denmark, France, Germany, Greece, Iceland, Ireland, Italy, Luxembourg, the Netherlands, Norway, Portugal, Spain, Sweden, Switzerland, Turkey, the United Kingdom and the United States. The following countries became Members subsequently through accession at the dates indicated hereafter: Japan (28th April 1964), Finland (28th January 1969), Australia (7th June 1971), New Zealand (29th May 1973), Mexico (18th May 1994) and the Czech Republic (21st December 1995). The Commission of the European Communities takes part in the work of the OECD (Article 13 of the OECD Convention).

Publié en français sous le titre :

DIVERSIFIER LES UTILISATIONS DES ÉTABLISSEMENTS SCOLAIRES

LES CAHIERS DU PEB

The Programme on Educational Building

The Programme on Educational Building (PEB) operates within the Organisation for Economic Co-operation and Development (OECD). Since its inception in 1972, PEB has promoted the international exchange of ideas, information, research and experience in all aspects of educational building.

PEB's priorities reflect the changing emphases of educational policy within participating countries. The overriding concerns of the Programme are to ensure that maximum educational benefit is obtained from past and future investment in educational buildings and equipment, and that the stock of facilities is planned and managed in the most effective and efficient way.

The three main themes of the Programme's work are:

- improving the quality and suitability of educational facilities and thus contributing to the quality of education;

- ensuring that the best possible use is made of the very substantial sums of money spent on constructing, running and maintaining educational facilities;

- giving early warning of the impact on educational facilities of trends in education and in society as a whole.

Also available

	France	Other countries*		
PEB Exchange (periodical) (88 00 00 1) ISBN 1018-9327, 1996 Subscription (3 issues)	FF 140	FF 160	US$ 34	DM 48
PEB Papers: Secondary Education in France, **A Decade of Change** (95 95 02 1) ISBN 92-64-14548-6, September 1995, 64 pp.	FF 70	FF 90	US$ 18	DM 26
Redefining the Place to Learn (95 95 03 1) ISBN 92-64-14563-X, August 1995, 172 pp.	FF 140	FF 180	US$ 37	DM 50
Schools for Cities (95 95 01 1) ISBN 92-64-14324-6, April 1995, 156 pp.	FF 100	FF 130	US$ 25	DM 39
PEB Papers: The Educational Infrastructure in Rural Areas (95 94 02 1) ISBN 92-64-14189-8, September 1994, 36 pp.	FF 40	FF 50	US$ 9	DM 16
PEB Papers: Educational Facilities for Special Needs (95 94 01 1) ISBN 92-64-14098-0, April 1994, 30 pp.	FF 40	FF 50	US$ 9	DM 16
Decentralisation and Educational Building Management: **The Impact of Recent Reforms** (95 92 01 1) ISBN 92-64-13660-6, October 1992, 84 pp.	FF 110	FF 140	US$ 28	DM 45
New Technology and its Impact on Educational Buildings (02 92 15 1) ISBN 92-64-13756-4, October 1992, 44 pp.	FF 40	FF 50	US$ 11	DM 16

* Export prices include dispatch via economic airmail.
THE OECD CATALOGUE OF PUBLICATIONS and supplements will be sent free
on request addressed either to the OECD Publications Service, or to the OECD distributor in your country.

Foreword

School buildings are expensive to construct and to maintain, yet many are used for only a few hours each day, and lie empty at weekends and during holidays. At the same time, there is a growing demand for facilities for lifelong learning, for leisure and for other community activities, while financial pressures on national and local authorities continue to grow.

In this context, the OECD Programme on Educational Building (PEB) and the French authorities organised a seminar in Lyon in 1995 which set out to identify the scope for broadening the use of educational facilities, inside and outside school hours.

This report presents the conclusions of the seminar, which was attended by experts from twenty OECD countries. It has been prepared for PEB by André Lafond, a General Inspector of the French Ministry of National Education. The ideas expressed are based on the discussions at the seminar and the documentation prepared for it, and do not necessarily represent the views of the national authorities concerned or those of the OECD. This report is published on the responsibility of the Secretary-General of the OECD.

Contents

Introduction

School premises and equipment represent a substantial investment of both capital and recurrent expenditure. But many buildings are used for a few hours only on school days and they very often remain empty during the holidays. In areas in which the population is decreasing, schools built in the past may be bigger than necessary, and consequently under-utilised.

At the same time, all countries are faced with a growing and changing demand for education. And, in social, economic, recreational and cultural fields, pressing new demands are emerging as a result of the technological, economic and sociological change affecting our societies.

The availability of premises and equipment together with the new demands and financial pressures on local authorities all point towards **broadening the use of school premises, both outside and during school hours,** to include different types of educational, community and other services.

To analyse this situation and address its implications, the OECD Programme on Educational Building (PEB), in conjunction with the French Ministry of National Education and with the participation of the Rhône-Alpes Region, Rhône Département and the city of Lyon, organised a seminar in Lyon from 29 to 31 March 1995 on the subject of "Broadening the Uses of Educational Buildings".

The background report to the seminar encouraged participants to focus on four main areas:

- child-care facilities and cultural and leisure activities for young people out of school hours;

- the organisation of social and cultural activities or further or continuing education courses for adults;

- the provision of resources and dissemination of information regarding new technology for small and medium-sized enterprises;

- the setting up of integrated community centres with the school as a focus for social and cultural activities, offering a village, neighbourhood or town a full range of services.

For each of these areas, participants were invited to consider the obstacles to extending the use of school accommodation, or the preconditions for success. Their attention was drawn in particular to the following problems:

- architectural: design and fitting out of premises; financial implications;

- responsibility and liability;

- operational: managing finances and human resources;

- organisational difficulties and possible resistance from the educational community, staff and parents;

- compatibility with the school's fundamental vocation, *i.e.* the education of children and adolescents.

This report aims to set out the main points of discussion fully and faithfully. A number of general comments can be made before going into detail on the issues.

Plurality and diversity

The solutions observed or investigated for broadening the uses of educational buildings vary from country to country and largely depend on cultural factors (what role does school play in society?), institutional factors (the degree of autonomy that schools have) and demographic, economic and social factors. Very different situations exist also within countries:

- areas of economic and population growth requiring the building of new schools, where new approaches can more easily be explored;

- declining rural or urban areas in the process of depopulation, where the process of restructuring a school and broadening its use is expected to make it a focus for the revival of the entire community;

- inner-city areas or suburbs experiencing serious social problems due to recession: unemployment, alienation of the immigrant population, youth unemployment and crime, violence, and drug-taking.

In deprived areas such as these, schools are one of the rare and sometimes only places where people who are becoming marginalised can be helped to resume their place in society.

There are therefore many aspects to the problem of expanding the use of educational buildings, which needs to be addressed in all its diversity and complexity.

Changing or expanding the use of educational buildings?

When a school or schools in the same neighbourhood no longer have enough pupils, the authorities may decide to close some or all of their buildings and use them for some other purpose: housing, shops, etc. Changing the use of schools in this way, is only marginally within the scope of the topic addressed by the seminar.

This process entails changing the use of educational buildings for economic reasons rather than extending their use as educational buildings. The seminar thus focused on the more usual and important case of a school remaining a school but having to accommodate and organise other educational, social, cultural or leisure activities on its premises in addition to teaching. Looked at in this way, extending the use of educational buildings widens a school's own remit and poses the problem of its role and place in its neighbourhood, town or village.

In addition to the purely economic logic of optimising the return from educational buildings and facilities, there is another, socially oriented logic which involves considering the social and cultural requirements of the community. It is not sufficient merely to consider the bare bones of the problem. A more general approach which includes the role of the school in society is required.

How far can we go?

To what extent can the role of the school be expanded without threatening its identity and jeopardising its fundamental vocation? Are there any limits which should not be transgressed?

Firstly, schools **alone** cannot meet all social needs. They do not have the necessary expertise and might be entering into competition with other specialist institutions. Having said that, schools can, and should, play a part in meeting the social needs of the area, whilst retaining their own identity. Any attention paid, for instance, to the out-of-school activities of young people, or lifelong education or information initiatives to help families, cannot fail to have a positive effect on school activities themselves.

Schools should not become businesses whose purpose is to maximise profits. In some cases, users pay for services, as in the case of adult continuing education or technology centres for small and medium-size enterprises. Schools can make a "profit" to spend on facilities for pupils or improving teaching aid. However, whilst it is justifiable to find ways to make extra money, there are certain limits. Too business-oriented an approach might detract the school head and teachers from their primary vocation.

Background and Issues

Factors contributing to under-utilisation

The most obvious and most general factor is the way school life is organised: classrooms are only occupied by pupils for a relatively short period each day and week, and schools are closed for holidays for two or three months of the year.

Demographic factors may also play a part, either through a general fall in the birth rate or through population movements causing a decline in school rolls in certain areas.

Thirdly, a country's education policy could reduce the number of schools through a series of mergers and amalgamations, making buildings available for other use.

Economic and social reasons for making better use of buildings

The economic reason is to obtain the best possible return on the money invested in building and running schools. The investment is even greater now that modern education requires larger accommodation (playing fields and special classrooms) and more sophisticated and expensive facilities: science laboratories, computer and audio-visual rooms, libraries, on-line access facilities, machine tools for vocational education. It would be unreasonable for group facilities such as these to be used by a single category of the population, and for a limited time.

In addition to this purely economic approach there are also general policy considerations concerning decentralisation and national and regional development.

The general trend in most countries is towards decentralisation. Central authorities are increasingly devolving responsibility to local authorities for the funding, organisation and management of public services directly affecting the local population, particularly education. The same trend extends to giving schools greater autonomy and scope for initiative. Local providers are better able to identify needs and resource availability; they are closer to the local population and answerable to it; the policy-making powers they are given permit greater administrative flexibility. The decentralisation measures introduced in various countries over the last few decades are not unconnected with the growing concern to rationalise the use of school resources.

On a national scale, the exodus from rural areas to towns and the decline in the industrial areas which had been highly prosperous in the nineteenth century are causing serious imbalances: whole areas are experiencing industrial decline and depopulation. Regional and national development policies are aimed at halting this process and establishing new poles of activity in threatened areas. Keeping schools open despite falling rolls is one aspect of these policies. School is often one of the last public services, if not the last, still remaining in a village with a declining population and its closure marks the symbolic and real death of the village. Making better use of school buildings could be a way of keeping not only the school but other public services too, such as the post office.

The emergence of new social needs

These new needs are many and varied:

- Higher standards of living and increased life expectancy in developed countries have instilled a desire to continue the learning process throughout life, enabling people to improve their minds, take up rewarding leisure activities, communicate and keep up with an ever-changing world.

- Rapid advances in knowledge and production methods for goods and services make a necessity of continuing to learn throughout life in order to keep their professional skills up to scratch. Parents, too, need to keep abreast of developments in order to stay on the same wavelength as their children and help them with their school work.

- The weakening of the family unit and widespread increase in the number of single-parent families and women at work mean that children and young people, as well as the elderly or disabled, now receive less attention and support within the family structure than before.

- In some countries, major population shifts have occurred through economic upheaval, resulting in a large reduction in the rural population and the hasty construction of souless suburbs with no social fabric. The isolation is even worse for immigrant populations which must contend with language and culture barriers.

- The recession has brought high unemployment to many countries, with disastrous results: poverty, marginalisation, crime, violence, drug abuse, etc. School leavers with no vocational qualifications looking for their first job are particularly vulnerable.

Faced with these increasing needs, the authorities have to provide new social services or improve existing ones. One way of doing this is to use resources available in the education sector, which are notoriously under-utilised. What makes this approach even more natural is that one of the main responses to the problems mentioned is to increase education provision for youngsters out of school hours and for adults generally. The problem is ultimately not only to broaden the use of educational buildings, but also to extend schools' educational remit to include other customers.

Unfortunately, the urgency or intensity of social needs does not necessarily coincide with availability, other than outside school hours and during holidays, of school buildings. In Florida (USA), for instance, demographic pressures mean that new schools have to be built at the same time as an intensive social programme is implemented. In Greece, lack of space is still forcing some schools to accept two shifts, one group of pupils in the morning and another in the afternoon.

Ways to improve the return on the use of educational buildings

The first option is to make economics the top priority, or the only priority, by closing down some or all of a school's buildings and using them for some other purpose to earn money. A school's maintenance costs will remain virtually the same whatever the size of the roll. If the decline in the roll results in a cut in the resources available to run the school, it is to the school's advantage to retrench and try to sell or rent some of its spare space for shops, flats or services.

The more usual approach, however, is to try to reconcile profitability and a response to the area's social needs by introducing the sharing or co-use of the school's facilities by several partners, either at different times (time split between school hours and out of school hours) or simultaneously, space permitting.

Co-use may take the form of a simple understanding between partners, each retaining control within its own sphere, with an agreement setting out the terms and conditions for sharing the facilities. It may also lead to genuine co-operation, with the various actors pooling their resources and together designing and implementing educational social projects. If this happens, it is most often the school that retains overall control of projects, or at least co-ordinates them.

Finally, the building of new towns or renovation of old and run-down urban areas and educational buildings can provide the impetus for **community learning centres** designed along appropriate architectural lines and combining on one site all the facilities required to meet the educational and social needs of the neighbourhood or town, offering wide opportunities for sharing use.

Several examples were given during the seminar, in particular:

- the Golden Grove Complex, located in a new suburb of Adelaide in South Australia;

- the Abraham Moss centre in Manchester (United Kingdom) set up to meet the needs of a deprived area in the course of renovation;

- the Dukeries Complex, also in the United Kingdom, designed to meet the needs of a small, rapidly declining mining town.

As a result of the combination of economic and social issues and the diversity of situations from country to country and within a single country, particularly in respect of decentralisation and regional and national development policies, there is a wide variety of cases to consider on the subject of extending the uses of school buildings.

A Wide Range of Actual and Possible Solutions

There are four main areas where the use of school buildings could be broadened:

- child-care facilities and cultural and leisure activities for children and young people out of school hours;

- the organisation of socio-cultural activities or further or continuing education for adults;

- information dissemination for small and medium-sized enterprises in respect of new technology;

- the setting up of integrated community centres, offering a whole range of social and educational services on the same site.

Facilities for very young children

Demand from families with very young children is for the provision of child-care, either for short periods – play groups – or for the whole day – nurseries. These facilities, usually organised by employers for their staff, or by local authority social services departments, require special equipment and qualified staff trained in child-care. Schools can accommodate services like these provided they have the space, buy the necessary equipment and recruit trained staff, but they seem rarely to do so because of the difficulties involved.

Examples quoted include the Dukeries Complex, which organises a *crèche* for parents taking part in the Complex's activities, and large universities, which provide nurseries for the children of their staff.

Most countries have some form of pre-school education for three to six-year olds (kindergarten, nursery schools), whether state or private, separate units or attached to a primary school. Although the purpose of these nursery schools is educational, they obviously do in fact also provide child-care, but only inside normal school hours, which is not what parents really need. Hence the demand for nursery schools to take children earlier in the morning and keep them later in the afternoon. That is relatively easy in terms of premises and equipment as nursery schools are already equipped to look after small children. The problem is recruiting extra staff and obtaining funding either from families or local authorities. Many such examples were reported, for instance from England, Sweden, Denmark and France.

Aside from the practicalities, the most important thing is the purpose of these services for parents and the spirit in which they are delivered. Nursery schools must not be reduced to being just short or long-stay "parking facilities". Broadening the provision for young children is obviously intended to help parents but it has another, more important, purpose and that is for school to become a real place of education and a forum for dialogue and exchange between families and teachers.

Activities for young people outside school hours

Young people and teenagers have a large amount of free time, outside school and after allowing for sleeping and eating. Parents do not always have the time or the means, nor the inclination, to supervise this free time. Left to their own devices, youngsters are exposed to idleness or activities that may be harmful to themselves and to society.

James Schroeer, from Florida, came up with an impressive list of the social problems affecting young people in the most deprived areas. Divorce, absentee fathers, illegitimate births, poverty, abuse and neglect gradually lead to underachievement, truancy then dropping out of school. The direct consequences are serial pregnancies, alcoholism, drug abuse and crime.

Even if the picture is not always so bleak, all countries are concerned to provide young people with leisure and cultural activities outside school hours which will help them to develop their personalities and improve their educational attainment.

Several initiatives were mentioned to deal with these problems.

Firstly, schemes to help pupils do their homework in the best possible conditions. There are many latchkey children who have no one at home to help them with their homework or supervise their activities. Guided study is organised for these children after school. Parents can ask for their children to stay and do their homework in comfortable surroundings with the assistance of a competent adult, either a teacher or volunteer parent. The problems these schemes raise are payment for staff and the children's transport arrangements, in rural or semi-rural locations. The authorities responsible for school transport will not readily consider organising two school runs, one for pupils leaving school at the normal time and another for those staying later.

As part of the policy to combat underachievement, directed study is widely recommended and practised in France, especially in underprivileged areas known as Zones of Educational Priority (ZEPs).

Secondly, the organisation of cultural, sporting or leisure activities in the lunch hour, in the afternoons if there are no lessons, on the weekly day off, if there is one, or at the weekend. Whether these activities are organised by the school itself or by outside associations or organisations, they all use the school's specialist facilities (sports fields, gymnasium, swimming pool, library, computer room, theatre, etc.).

Of particular note in this respect is the pilot "All-day schools" scheme launched in Greece in 560 nursery and primary schools. Lessons are given in the mornings from 08:00 to 12:00 and pupils are offered a wide range of further activities from 07:00 to 08:00 in the morning and from 12:00 to 16:00, or 16:30, in the afternoon, designed to develop their imagination, creativity, sensitivity, initiative and communication skills. These activities are supervised by teachers who are from the school or specially recruited for this job. The scheme is funded by the State, local authorities and parents' associations.

Finally, the organisation of activities to keep children occupied during the school holidays, especially the long summer break. Children in deprived areas do not have the money to use these holidays to travel, with or without their families. A possible solution is to use schools, as these are empty during the holidays. A good example is the "Open School" project launched in France in June 1991 by the Ministry of Social Affairs and Integration and the Ministry of Education. The purpose of the operation is to enable youngsters deprived of holidays to spend their free time profitably and enjoyably. The operation is designed for secondary schools which volunteer, and which are invited to offer youngsters from underprivileged areas a programme of educational, cultural, school, sporting and leisure activities. The operation was designed to combat both marginalisation and educational failure. The youngsters are directly involved in the design, preparation and overall management of the programme of activities, which is a key to its success. The adults involved are teachers who volunteer, local authority officials, members of associations, parents of pupils, and university students. They are all entitled to remuneration.

Ever since it was launched, the operation has been very successful. It has now been extended to some fifteen educational districts (*Académies*). Essentially, it is designed for children from large families of foreign origin with low incomes.

Adult continuing education

Adult initiatives fall into three categories:

- those seeking to provide opportunities for personal development in areas directly connected to a person's work;

- those which aim at improvement, advancement or training in a person's occupation;

- those which try to help the unemployed and young people to find work or obtain a professional qualification to help them enter or re-enter the labour market.

The first set of initiatives is based on the philosophy that education is not just for school-aged children, but also for men and women **throughout their whole life,** in other words that education should be a **lifelong process.**

Increased life expectancy and higher living standards in developed countries mean that more time can be devoted to leisure, sporting, cultural or intellectual activities. The rapid strides in learning, changing life-styles, the internationalisation of relations and the advent of a communications society have all served to create very high demand in this area, all the higher still in that initial education standards are continuously rising. In addition to this demand there are the more specific needs of certain groups of the population which schools cannot afford to ignore.

All the countries represented at the seminar have recognised this need and all provided specific examples. Jean-Louis Derouet quoted from the French Education Act of 10 July 1989, that "continuing education is part of the mission of schools".

The many examples included the following:

- Initiatives for the elderly: keep-fit classes, social and leisure clubs, artistic activities (day centre for older people in the Dukeries Complex, universities of the third age, etc.).

- Language courses for international travel and business.

- Computer courses for beginners.

- Distance-learning.

- Initiatives targeted at parents, grand-parents and other adults concerned to help them to understand and support children in their school work. In underprivileged areas, academic achievement is directly dependent on raising the skills and awareness of parents. This is even more vital in the case of immigrant populations suffering from illiteracy and poor knowledge of the host country's language.

Continuing vocational training

The rapid changes in technology and in the production methods of goods and services oblige employees to undergo vocational training throughout their lifetime in order to keep their skills up to scratch, keep up to date with changes and remain competitive in the labour market. Whilst demand may come from individuals themselves, it is usually firms which request and pay for courses of this type. A market in continuing vocation training has therefore grown up and is continuing to expand. Schools, particularly vocational and technical schools, possess the human and equipment resources to meet this demand.

Whilst the participation of schools in continuing vocational training is observed in a number of countries, it is perhaps in France that it is the most developed. Legislation was introduced in 1971 making it compulsory for firms to spend a percentage of their wage bill on in-service training for their staff. Secondary schools are permitted to assist in providing this training, in return for payment and on a competitive basis. Since 1974, they have taken the initiative to offer training to firms or individuals tailored to their requirements. To do this, they have formed school establishment groups – called GRETAs – linked by heads of agreement detailing their respective responsibilities, with a view to sharing their equipment and staff resources and marketing high quality education.

The income thus obtained enables the schools to pay the teachers who offer their services and also to improve, sometimes considerably, their own finances. State secondary schools have together become the largest continuing training provider in the country. GRETAs had a FF 3 billion turnover in 1993. They had 1 300 training consultants and 7 625 permanent trainers, in addition to which 37 000 teachers gave continuing training classes over and above their normal teaching commitments.

There are limits in practice: the time spent by school heads responsible for GRETAs in prospecting markets and by teachers giving in-service training should not adversely affect their duties towards their pupils, but rather should help to open up the school to the world of work. It has also been found necessary to abandon a supply-led approach in favour of a demand-led approach to ensure that training courses continue to match individual needs and requirements.

Initiatives to facilitate access to the labour market

A range of initiatives has been taken by schools to help the unemployed and school leavers without jobs, including the following:

- In the Dukeries Complex in England, a centre run by the unemployed for the unemployed offers opportunities for unemployed adults to come together for support, to exchange knowledge and share information. There is also a Job Club organised by employment services offering training in job search and interview techniques.

- Full-Service Schools in Florida assist people on welfare to enter the labour market (Project Independence) and, in collaboration with the Department of Labor and Employment Security, try to improve placement services for students from vocational and technical schools.

- In France, "qualification contracts" are offered to unemployed youngsters who left school without any qualifications. These young people do part-time paid work for a firm whilst at the same time pursuing in-school education leading to a recognised qualification. The aim is the consolidation of basic knowledge whilst developing personal plans for finding employment.

Schools as technology dissemination centres

The concept of schools as a centre of technology dissemination, not only to pupils but also to firms and craftsmen, as a means of promoting new developments, is not new. As far back as the late eighteenth century the authors of education plans, inspired by the philosophy of Enlightenment and the Encyclopaedia spirit, thought that "schools were to put the peasants and craftspeople in touch with the new procedures and machines which were beginning to change the world of production".[1]

Numerous examples of this extended role of the school were quoted during the seminar. In Scotland and Sweden, in sparsely populated areas, schools provide introductory computer courses for farmers and small traders to enable them to modernise their operations. In Quebec, the vocational education centres are designed as "technology showcases for the business community. Some provide industry-oriented facilities, such as assay and test laboratories".[2]

In France, strong emphasis is placed on the concept of the school as a centre of activity for the dissemination of technology to small and medium-sized firms, mainly in low growth areas. Schools offering vocational and technical training have expensive, up-to-date equipment since they have to give their pupils a theoretical and practical education based on the latest technology. Small firms, on the other hand, often have older equipment due to lack of financial resources. Isolated firms find it difficult to

---

1.   Jean-Louis Derouet, *Opening up the school: some reflections on the French experience.*

2.   Luc Desgagnés, *Broadening the uses of school buildings in Quebec.*

keep abreast of technological innovations and this could impair their competitiveness. If firms are weakened or even pushed out of business as a result, there would be an even greater risk of decline in rural and semi-rural areas, hence the desire to introduce a partnership between schools and business in the field of technological innovation.

This is the result of a positive trend which, for the last twenty years in France, has been bringing the school and business communities together. A significant factor in this has been the participation of schools in adult continuing education, as described above, and also the development of alternating classroom/workplace training whereby pupils undertake training in firms whilst still at school. Here the opposite process applies. Managers and workers visit schools to discover new manufacturing methods, new machinery and possibly how to make use of them.

This partnership may go beyond mere demonstration or provision of the school's most sophisticated equipment and lead to genuine co-operation. At firms' requests, pupils, assisted by their teachers, plan and produce studies, projects and prototypes. The school plays a role similar to that of the university or private laboratories which the enterprise would approach if it were not so remote. Services are paid for either in money or equipment and open up very good employment opportunities for the pupils. Patents may be involved in some cases.

The Cibeins agricultural school near Lyon illustrates this policy. The school and the farm attached to it play an important role in technological progress and dissemination of research findings in the field of aquaculture which assist in developing the immediate area which is rich in lakes and ponds. There are three priority aims: experimentation, demonstration and dissemination of results. The school also has a piscicultural documentation centre that is unrivalled anywhere in France and can be used by businesses and researchers.

The last school in the village

In rural areas experiencing depopulation, the school is often the last remaining public service, "a symbol of the village's survival". The prospect of its closure due to insufficient pupils is seen as a catastrophe and provokes a great deal of protest – sometimes violent protest – by the population. Using the empty space for other services (library, post office, bank, etc.) may be a way of saving the school, keeping some life in the village and preventing the inhabitants from moving away. Examples of this happening in the mountainous regions of Austria were cited.

One example among many is the school at Batiscan, Quebec, which the *Samuel de Champlain* school board decided to close. "As soon as the decision was announced, students' parents organised a boycott movement... Parents' determination forced the various levels of government to work together to find a solution to keep the school open, use it more efficiently and share the costs between various organisations. The municipality decided to move the municipal library into the empty space in the school, thus reducing some of the costs borne by the school board. The community rallied to find a solution."[3]

Integrated community centres

In his paper,[4] Michael Hacker pointed out that the idea of designing and building community centres bringing together on the same site, using shared facilities, many of the educational and social services which the population of a neighbourhood or small town might require, is not new. This approach, used in England for fifty years, received a new lease of life in the 1960s and '70s when it was encouraged by central government and adopted by local education authorities. The example has been repeated since, with varying degrees of success, in numerous countries including France and the Netherlands.

These centres offer all the services already mentioned – childcare facilities and youth leisure

3. Luc Desgagnés, *Ibid.*

4. Michael Hacker, *Two decades of school and community collaboration in the United Kingdom.*

activities, adult further and continuing education, technology dissemination centres, etc. – but with a more systematic, results-oriented approach. The schools mentioned to date used their empty space to accommodate various services for which they were not originally designed, something which required adaptations, imposed constraints and ultimately limited the options available. Community centres, on the other hand, built when a new neighbourhood or town is being constructed or an old neighbourhood or old school rebuilt or renovated, are designed from the outset to bring together, accommodate and operate the widest variety of services on the same site in purpose-built and equipped buildings. Whilst priority is given to educational services and meeting social needs, the presence of services of an administrative (local authority) or quasi-administrative (post office, bank) nature and even of shops, *cafés*, restaurants or accommodation facilities is not ruled out.

According to Michael Hacker, "the concept of community school embraces three main principles:

- Education is a continuous lifelong process and is not confined to the childhood years of compulsory education.

- Educational attainment is closely related to the support and understanding of parents and the wider community. This indicates a need to remove the walls, both physical and institutional, that tend to separate schools from the societies they serve.

- There are significant economic advantages to be gained from the joint provision and more intensive use of school and community facilities."[5]

Several examples of community centres could be cited. The three mentioned below each have different features:

- the full-service schools in Florida;

- the Golden Grove Complex in South Australia;

- the Dukeries Complex in the north of England.

Full-service schools in Florida

The full-service schools in Florida are characterised not so much by the concern to share the use of school premises as by an urgent social need in certain areas to provide health, social, and employment services from the school.

According to the paper presented and analysed by H. James Schroeer, "a **full-service** school means a school which serves as a **central point of delivery,** a 'community hub', for whatever education, health, social, human and/or employment services have been determined locally to be needed to support a child's and a family's success in school and in the community". The services which it offers are integrated "in locations which are easily accessible". They should be "an extension of the education process, yet be integrated to the point where all players feel a part of, and understand their role in, the overall programme".[6]

Full-service schools are set up in areas where children are, or are at risk of becoming, victims of social problems. Given the complexity of the problems to be resolved and the number of organisations involved, "the public school facility seems a logical site" as "the school site is one of many possible sites where health, social, education and employment services may be co-located to best serve a community".

The many different support services that can be offered in these schools vary according to what is needed locally, but include:

- parenting programmes,

- adult education,

- employment services,

- housing assistance,

- health care,

- child-care programmes,

---

5. Michael Hacker, *ibid.*

6. H. James Schroeer, *Full-service schools: a Florida perspective.*

- delinquency prevention,

- substance abuse prevention.

Golden Grove Complex in South Australia

Golden Grove is a new suburb on the outskirts of Adelaide, South Australia. Commenced in 1984, Golden Grove expects to have a population of 30 000 by its completion in 1998. One of the primary objectives of the planners of the new suburb was to deliver a full range of human services **from the very beginning** and special attention was paid to education, which was considered of central importance.

A resolutely new approach led to the construction of the Golden Grove Secondary School Complex. The complex is centrally located on a 25 hectare site within the Golden Grove development and contains three secondary schools (a state high school, a Catholic college and a Protestant college), an adult education centre and a cultural and leisure centre. Each school has individual discrete buildings with individual playing areas, but all three **share facilities:** on-line library facilities and central library; technical and technology workshops covering wood, metal and plastics; special facilities for music, drama, home economics, information technology, science, etc. The schools not only share these facilities but share teachers, enabling a broad curriculum to be offered. Greater provision of education for children with special needs, language teaching and vocational training is also possible than would be the case in stand-alone schools.

This innovative project had a number of objectives:

- Firstly, through the principle of co-use of facilities and careful planning of work right from the start, to achieve savings in both capital investment and running costs.

- Secondly, to give this new suburb a soul and community spirit, thereby avoiding the risks of isolation and social fragmentation and the trouble this could cause; the Golden Grove Complex offers people a unifying symbol of co-operation in the place that they live.

- Finally, to change the traditional relationship between schools and the community and open the school to the community. Education is now a process which occurs as much at home and in the workplace as at school.

The Dukeries Complex in England

The Dukeries Complex is an example of a school under-used, due to a declining enrolment, being converted at low cost for community use. The village of Ollerton (Nottinghamshire), where the Dukeries Comprehensive School is situated, is located in a rapidly declining mining area. The community needed to find a solution to the economic crisis and its accompanying social problems.

The Dukeries Comprehensive School was built in 1964 on a campus which has excellent playing fields, physical education and recreation provision, workshops, and science and craft facilities. It had a residential centre and had over the years built up a rural science unit. It was conceived originally as a community school and contained a 200-seat theatre, concert hall and youth club.

There was a considerable drop in enrolment from 1970 to 1982 and a further fall was expected. The question then arose as to what to do with the spare space which was proving expensive to maintain.

The views of the local people were sought, culminating in a report entitled "A Place for the Family" and a blueprint for converting 4 000 m² of spare space (which cost £80 000 per annum to heat, light and maintain) into facilities needed by the community. "The Complex now embraces a community college, a recreation centre, a 25-bed residential centre, an under-5's centre, a purpose-built youth centre, a public/school library and

---

7. Roy Sowden, *The Dukeries Complex: a place for the family.*

information centre, an agency centre (mini town hall), a school/public cafeteria, a day centre for the elderly, an adult training centre for adults with learning difficulties, an adult unemployed centre and a Fire Brigade Training Centre."[7]

The Complex has now been in existence for ten years, and its success can be measured by the support it attracts from the local community, the increasing participation in education post 16 and the relatively low crime rate.

The Keys to Success

It can be seen that there are many different ideas as to how to broaden the use of educational buildings to include other services. But not all projects are successfully completed, and some have difficulty in functioning properly or in surviving for any length of time. What are the conditions which ensure that such projects work? What are the keys to success?

The answers to these questions may be grouped under three headings: **conception, management, communication.** Projects have to be coherent, and anticipate problems. They must be put into effect and administered in accordance with strict management rules, from both a financial and a personnel viewpoint. And above all, they must be such as to be able, at all times, to convince and attract the support of the decision-makers, actors, users and all members of the local community.

A good project

Broadening the uses of school premises – whether new buildings or existing ones – to include purposes other than the education of children is possible only if a coherent project has first been formulated, a project which covers all the architectural aspects, anticipates all foreseeable consequences, is guaranteed to function smoothly and, last but not least, allows worthwhile savings to be made. This applies to small-scale projects for the partial and temporary use of premises, as well as to large-scale ones, such as the construction of a community education centre.

First of all, the project must be credible and able to attract the support of those with the power to sanction and finance it.

When a new site is being developed – as at Golden Grove – those in charge are tempted to provide for welfare facilities, including schools, gradually, as and when new inhabitants move in, which may extend over a period of five or six years. The primary concern of the authors of the project was to show that, contrary to received wisdom, building educational premises **at the very beginning** was proof of a coherent project and would enable substantial savings to be made. Quite apart from the commercial argument – the existence of schools from the outset makes it easier to sell apartments – the promoter recognised that including future schools in the initial excavation and servicing work made for savings since it enabled better co-ordination and a more rational use of construction equipment. He accepted these arguments and in this way helped finance the schools.

To help get the "Dukeries Complex" project accepted and also to encourage new ideas concerning it, Roy Sowden took care to consult the local population. During a week of activities christened "Tell us about Ollerton", the members of the working party created on this occasion, joined by officers from the Architects Department and Buildings Group at the Department of Education, invited members of the public, informed of events by advertising or personal telephone calls, to come and give their views about Ollerton and its needs.

In similar vein, when a new high school is being built in France, it is now common practice to appoint the new principal one year in advance so that he can participate in the project with the architects and the project manager, consult the future users, act as their interpreter *vis-à-vis* those in charge, follow the work and intervene if necessary.

In general, it is helpful to associate future users and members of the local community with projects.

The project must take account of all the architectural aspects. The primary requirement in this field is to design buildings which can be adapted easily to a variety of uses, whether simultaneous or consecutive. It is difficult to predict future numbers of school children in a given area. A new neighbourhood will attract young couples, the parents of young children. If they are happy there, they will remain, as they and their children grow older; primary schools will grow empty as secondary schools fill up before becoming too big in their turn. The same pattern applies to movements of populations from the countryside to the towns or from city centres to the suburbs. Any design for a new school or school complex must now take account of this demographic evolution and provide, from the outset, for other later uses for the premises in question, such as shops or housing.

New projects must also incorporate imaginative architectural features permitting the co-use of premises and avoiding friction between different groups of users, or alternatively, allowing consecutive uses in the same building: for example, a school can be used as a residential and recreation centre during the summer holidays. At the Abraham Moss Centre in Manchester, (United Kingdom), the sloping site was turned to advantage to make a separate entrance to each of the three levels of the building, providing different groups of users with their own ground-level access off pedestrian streets.

As regards the necessary "flexibility" in the use of school buildings, the various architectural approaches have advantages and disadvantages. The choice of small separate units seems to offer the greatest flexibility of use, but has the disadvantage of being expensive in terms of capital investment and running costs (greater surface area and higher maintenance costs). The use of temporary modular buildings which can be dismantled and transported does not enjoy unanimous support. Transformation, dismantling and re-erecting operations are never as easy as they are supposed to be; they are expensive and accelerate the process of wear and tear.

While flexibility is recognised by everyone as an objective, ways in which to achieve it vary. It is, on the other hand, relatively easy to draw up a generally agreed list of the minimum conditions to be met to make the co-use of school buildings by different groups as easy as possible.

- **Access to, and movement within, the premises:** there is no problem if adults and children, or different groups of adults, can be given separate means of access and areas in which to conduct their activities. This requires a clear and explicit system of signposting. Examples were given of cases in which the system for the day-time separation of children and adults was removed in the evening, when only adults remained.

- **Comfortable conditions for all groups:** soundproofing is important when several groups are using premises at the same time. Furnishings also have to be suitable and provision made for additional space for services and administration, storage, bigger and more appropriate toilet facilities, increased maintenance services, and rooms suitable for use by groups of different size.

- **Safety of persons and property:** requirements here are for an appropriate caretaking service, suitable instructions in the event of fire, and the provision of additional emergency exits.

Lastly, the question of cost has to be borne in mind. Be it to adapt old buildings or to construct new ones, the costs involved are always high. The first consideration for the authors of a project is to ensure the necessary funding. In the case of large-scale projects, such as a community education centre, funding has inevitably to come from various sources, involving several bodies or authorities and numerous procedures. When funds are scarce, a project must first and foremost demonstrate its relevance and show that, if accepted, it will bring long-term savings.

In particular, it must be shown that the financial benefits expected from the sharing of premises and equipment will not be offset by an increase in the cost of the work required and in operating costs. If these concerns are taken into account at the design stage, it should be possible to achieve the desired result. Various approaches are possible. A modular design makes it possible for security, cleaning, lighting, heating or air conditioning to be limited to those areas actually used and for the duration of their use only, something which reduces running costs considerably. Similarly, the systematic use of new technology means that timetables and the use of premises, energy and water consumption, a continual assessment of running costs and the regular monitoring of expenditure and income can all be administered by computer, or means that access to, and movement within the premises can be monitored more easily with the help of TV cameras.

Good management

Management can be looked at in terms of financing and in terms of organisation.

The more schools open up to other users, the more complex and difficult become the problems of financing. As the Director of the Dukeries Complex Community Centre said, "our most difficult problem is the way we are now funded from nine major different sources". This multiple dependence gives a certain fragility to the whole, "a house of cards" to use the expression adopted by Roy Sowden.

When a school organises or provides accommodation for services other than educational ones, with a shared use of premises and equipment, this generates additional running, maintenance and depreciation costs. Good management would dictate that these costs should

be met by corresponding income, otherwise it is the budget, and therefore the running, of the school which loses out in the long term. The users of the new services offered must therefore make a financial contribution at least equal to the real cost of those services. In exchange for their goodwill and the additional, though not always visible, work involved in this opening towards the outside, schools can even legitimately make a small profit in order to improve their teaching aids and the conditions of work for pupils and staff. Couched in these terms, the problem appears simple. In practice, it is not.

The first difficulty is the uncertain nature of some financial sources. If a school provides or accommodates services of a social nature, the most disadvantaged users are not always able to pay the real cost involved, and sometimes they are not charged anything. The difference is made up by subsidies or grants from government departments, local authorities or various associations. But the fact that these subsidies are awarded annually, and not always renewed, complicates the task of the school and makes its functioning more precarious. In such circumstances, certain schools may hesitate to launch large-scale projects, or prefer to limit themselves to contractual-type operations on an annual basis, as for example for the "École ouverte" operation in France, referred to above. The more ambitious projects, such as the 'Dukeries Complex', are obliged to make a constant effort of communication – which will be referred to below – to prove the worth of their activities, and convince those holding funds to continue to give their support.

The second difficulty is how to assess the real cost of the service provided. To what extent can the head of a school be expected to act as a managing director? There is a tendency for those who have not been trained in management techniques to underestimate the costs involved and not to take into account all the expenditure required, for example by forgetting or not knowing how to evaluate electricity consumption for evening activities, or the extra work required of caretakers or cleaning staff. Such oversights will in the end of the day be charged to the school's operating budget. Failure to take account of maintenance and depreciation costs is the owners' responsibility.

If the owner is a local authority, this may be a deliberate choice within the context of a wider policy, though this choice must be explicit and made known.

When schools are in competition with others with regard to services provided, for example, continuing education for adults or specialised work carried out for companies, under-charging raises a fundamental problem: private organisations supplying similar services will, justifiably, feel themselves to be the victims of unfair competition.

It is therefore important to estimate the real cost of services resulting from the broadening of the uses of educational buildings, and failure to do so will give rise to problems. A basic management principle is to identify costs with those who incur the costs. But can we go further and expect such services to make a profit for the school and those working in it? This is a legitimate goal if it allows the school to fulfil its vocation in better conditions. There is, however, an obvious risk that the school, by this means, is turned insidiously into a profit-making enterprise. Doubtless the existence of rules, the vigilance of those in charge and, above all, their professional conscience and sense of pedagogical responsibility help school heads and teachers to resist such tendencies.

From the organisational viewpoint, several questions arise: Who decides? Who does what? Who is responsible? How can the best use be made of the time, space, resources and skills available?

If the many activities taking place in a school are to be properly co-ordinated, there has to be a management body, and roles and tasks have to be clearly defined. Generally speaking, responsibility for conducting operations seems to fall to the school head, and this seems both reasonable and efficient. However, an examination of what happens in practice reveals several different types of approach.

In France, a formal contract must be drawn up between the school, the owner of the premises, the mayor of the commune and the future user, for each case of use, whether occasional or regular, by outside partners. This contract lays down the obligations, responsibilities and the sharing of costs between the school and the outside user who, however, remains in control of his activity: for example, a gymnastics club which uses the school gymnasium for its members. In such cases, the school does no more than provide facilities for the activities of an outside organisation. This is not the case, however, for continuing education or instruction in technological know-how organised and given by the school itself: there is of course an agreement with one or more outside partners, but this agreement relates to the nature of the service expected and not to the sharing of the premises. In such cases, it is the school head who plays the role of initiator, director and organiser.

In some countries, essentially in cases where integrated community centres are to be found in which organisations of different types co-habit and co-operate on a permanent basis, the complexity of the system leads to the creation of a joint administrative and supervisory body.

At the Regional Centre for Initiatives in Agricultural Training (CRIFA) of Coaticook (Quebec), a management board was set up with four members designated by the CIARC (Centre for agricultural projects for the Coaticook Region) board and four members by the school board.

At the Dukeries Complex, the campus director, managers of functional units and the central management team constitute a policy council known as the "Campus Office Group".

Generally speaking, the management body must ensure that:

- the share of each group of users with respect to the functioning of the whole is clearly defined;

- the management of time and space is both strict (full use) and responsible (premises and equipment treated properly);

- the allocation of tasks and responsibilities is clear and well-known;

- safety measures are complied with;

- insurance is taken out in respect of accidents and possible damage.

Strong motivation and good communication

However innovative and ingenious the project, however strict and efficient the management, broadening the uses of school buildings cannot succeed without the strong support of the actors involved, the users and the members of the community in general, without forgetting those who control possible sources of funding. This support will be based on the one hand on the personal qualities, competence and motivation of the school head, and on the other, on an active communications policy.

Introducing changes into an organisation causes perturbation and can generate reactions of fear, or rejection, on the part of its members. Teaching and non-teaching staff may be tempted to defend "their" territory; parents can raise objections. As stressed by seminar participants, there has to be a broadening of the mind of school staff and partners before any broadening of the uses of the premises is possible. It was also said that the attitude of the people involved and the values to which they are attached no doubt constitute the greatest restriction.

To overcome such resistance and dispel any suspicion, we have to inform, explain, reassure, and show to teachers, parents, pupils and managers, the advantages, including financial benefits, that the school can expect from a broadening of this type. Indeed, such tendencies have to be reversed and the support of all those concerned has to be obtained. In this endeavour of communication, the motivation, determination and charisma of the school head are vital. As James Schroeer said, "a school will become a full-service school only with the support and commitment of school management, parents and the community".

Information campaigns must not be limited to the period when initiatives are launched, but must be continued permanently in order to ensure the best possible conditions for the development of projects and to guarantee their survival.

It can be difficult, and give rise to problems, for staff of different origins and with different skills to live and work together unless such cohabitation and co-operation have been carefully prepared in advance. Training courses, the setting up of liaison groups, and the appointment of a "mediator" are all solutions which have been proposed. The time should be taken to listen to the opinion of each person concerned and to take it into account. If results are assessed and difficulties identified, it should be possible in a spirit of co-operation, to adapt a project which has already been started as and when necessary in order to avoid any pitfalls which had not been anticipated and to make full use of unexpected positive results. The paper from Florida[8] states in this respect that programmes will inevitably evolve, over time, as and when the different partners get to know each other better, obstacles are defined and overcome, new resource possibilities identified, the effectiveness of services assessed and changes made in consequence.

Lastly, schools offering broader uses must advertise their existence and their success. The information given to the outside world in general, families, partners and local authorities must be abundant, clear and perfectly transparent.

Schools, whose sources of financing are always precarious, will guarantee the survival of initiatives they undertake if they:

- identify and advertise the educational and material benefits, advantages and profits involved;

- publish reports;

- associate, in the organisation of the new activities, all those with an interest in the outcome;

- promote, on the basis of duly evaluated results, the activities undertaken.

---

8. H. James Schroeer, *Full-service schools: a Florida perspective.*

How Far Can The Broadening of Uses of Educational Buildings be Taken?

How far can the broadening of the use of educational buildings be taken without endangering the school's identity? Are there limits which ought not to be crossed, beyond which the primary vocation of schools – the instruction and education of children and teenagers – is in danger of being compromised? These questions reflect a feeling that schools must ensure that teaching remains at the heart of any new venture, and that schools cannot tackle all society's problems. Is there a risk that broadening the uses of educational buildings will aim exclusively at solving social problems to the detriment of teaching?

This cautious or even suspicious approach to new activities is based on experience and refers to arguments which merit analysis.

What limits?

The concept of a limit is ambivalent. It includes obstacles and resistance to be overcome in order to implement a project, as well as values or ideals which must not be compromised. Those who speak of limits to new activities are not immune to this ambivalence: invoking the relative failure of integrated facility projects, the physical threats to schools in certain inner-city or suburban areas with a very poor social environment, or the unsettling business of trying to obtain funds, they do not distinguish between

these difficulties or risks which must be identified and avoided, and the fundamental principles of the school which must in no case be compromised.

Integrated school projects, as launched in a number of countries in the 1960s and 70s, sometimes had problems in developing, and some failed. As seen above, the basic idea behind them was to create centres open to all in which, on the same premises, educational, cultural and social services would be provided for all sections of the population. But very often, this "idealistic" vision came up against management difficulties and the resistance of the different actors called upon to share the same premises, each tending to protect his territory and keep his old habits. In some cases, where projects were insufficiently thought through, initial ambitions had to be gradually reduced. This process is well described in a document from the Netherlands: "When interviewing people who are involved in the construction of those multi-functional buildings in the 60s and 70s, it occurred to me they had dropped a great deal of their social ideals and had become more practical. Different socio-cultural institutions in those former multi-functional buildings built walls between spaces that used to be open to everybody. If they feel more comfortable having their own spaces, we just let them. It seems the gap between the events for the elderly and for instance child-care is too wide to overcome. Smoking cigars and playing cards are no lucky combination with playing children. So that the only thing in common is the owner and manager of the complex. The character of the co-operation between different socio-cultural institutions has been reduced to a merely economical instead of an idealistic co-operation".[9]

In some cases too, management difficulties themselves proved insurmountable and caused the project to fail.

Such examples of failure should not, however, call into question the broadening of the uses of educational buildings. At most, they show what precautions should be taken to ensure success. As seen above, a coherent project, strong motivation, full support, the permanent participation of the different actors involved, good communication and open management are necessary Where these conditions have not been fully met, difficulties have arisen.

Analysing the failure of integrated facilities, Jean-Louis Derouet, in his paper, gives a more "political" explanation, but one which also stresses the need for strong local involvement: "The fashion of integrating facilities was based on a model defined by national and international experts who wished to make the most efficient use of cultural facilities in the new cities. This rationality was imposed on the population. Integrated facilities, through their spatial layout, were to force establishments to open up. In a way, this involved manipulating the different groups concerned by forcing them to meet and co-operate through the overlapping of spaces. Beyond the fact that the conditioning effect of space has yet to be proven, the resourcefulness of people in escaping this type of constraint knows no bounds. Everywhere the number of reinforced doors were multiplied, justified by unquestionable safety needs, putting an end to the intermingling of spaces. Nowadays everything is based on legal agreements, that is, the concerted action of the parties involved: contracts with the municipality, accords between the school and the enterprise, and so on. Even though the work of will requires time, and can fail, it is people who rule things and not the contrary".[10]

Problems of security are another reason for reluctance to open up school premises. Many schools built in the 1970s in an open style, without any fencing which, due to a deterioration in the social environment, are today at risk of outside aggression which is a threat to persons – teachers and pupils – as well as to the buildings themselves. In what would seem to be a step backwards, premises which had been designed to be open must today, for reasons of safety, be protected by solid fencing and placed under a strict surveillance system. A vocational school in the Lyon area, built cheek by jowl with flats and shops, is one example. Today, relations between the local inhabitants and pupils have deteriorated to such an extent that, to avoid trouble, the shopkeepers prefer to close their shutters when the children are let out of school. In another, extreme, case, a college built in the early 1970s alongside and integrated with apartment blocks, recently had to be demolished because of operational difficulties, and replaced by a traditional-type building.

There is no doubt that the recession has in certain areas been accompanied by social disintegration to such a degree that the most basic rules of community living have been disrupted or even disappeared altogether. The rule of law has been replaced by relations based on force, violence and crime. In such circumstances, school buildings that are open "physically" become a target and, paradoxically, the first concern and duty of such a school is to protect itself and its pupils from outside threats. In these so-called "sensitive" neighbourhoods, schools are sometimes the only places in which the law is still respected and where children can, in an atmosphere of peace and safety, relearn the meaning of social values and the rules of community life.

But can "sanctuary" schools remain indifferent to local developments and turn in on themselves? In some areas, the liberal projects of the 1970s are now facing social problems which were not foreseen. The ideal of physical openness has had to come to terms with reality, but should

---

9. Harriet Sinnige, *Broadening the use of educational buildings: Dutch experiences.*

10. Jean-Louis Derouet, *Opening up the school: some reflections on the French experience.*

schools use this as a pretext for restricting their vocation to the "disembodied" transmission of learning and know-how? It would seem, on the contrary, that in such extreme cases which, happily, are rare in all countries, schools can and must even more than elsewhere act as a social crucible and work, together with the other social actors, to repair the social fabric.

However, the openness of premises has too often been confused with the openness of a school towards its environment. There is an "openness of mind" which can survive even if temporary constraints mean that the school walls have to be maintained or reinforced. The same applies to the co-use of school premises: the fact of co-use does not necessarily mean that all physical separations have to be abolished.

Another objection is that schools engaged in too many activities run the risk of over-diversification and speculation. This applies essentially when a school is not content to share its premises or to act as host to other users, but itself organises a whole series of activities of a social or cultural nature. This requires an additional effort on the part both of the management and of the teachers, to collect together the necessary skills and financing, and to administer the whole.

Whether the activities involved are social ones subsidised by central or local government, or services paid for by the recipients (individuals, associations or firms), there is no escaping the need to balance a complex budget: schools then become veritable businesses which must constantly strive to maintain their activities at the level desired. This no doubt creates an atmosphere of great energy but it may be wondered whether it is desirable for a school head to become an entrepreneur taken up with countless outside concerns to the point perhaps of no longer being able to give the necessary time and attention to the teaching and education of his pupils.

In some cases, additional activities undertaken by a school can bring in precious financial resources which can be used to improve school equipment or the working conditions of pupils and teachers. But how far along this road is it possible to go without transforming the school into a profit-making enterprise? Money matters become more delicate still when extra work done by the school head or by teachers has to be remunerated, thus giving them extra income over and above their normal salary. In some cases, this can no doubt lead to the temptation to accept too many "outside" remunerated tasks to increase personal income, to the detriment of the "ordinary" work for which the persons concerned were trained and appointed.

These are certainly real risks. However, they can clearly be avoided by establishing rules of conduct and complying with a code of ethics: nothing should be accepted which can prejudice a school's primary vocation and the quality of its teaching.

The problem of limits to be respected applies also in relation to what activities can be conducted within school premises. But if proper precautions are taken, any fears or objections should be dispelled. In no case did the reticence encountered call into question the actual principle of broadening the use of educational buildings. Opening up schools is a difficult exercise which requires certain precautions, but this must not serve as an excuse or pretext for turning inwards. What is more, opening up in this way is no doubt both inevitable and very profitable for schools themselves.

Opening to the outside: an inevitable and rewarding process

Today, at the end of the twentieth century, there seems no longer any place for the concept of a school devoted to the instruction and education of a particular age group – children and teenagers – in a self-contained space, protected from outside influences. Several factors have contributed to this inevitable development:

- The prolongation of studies means that schools increasingly play host to young adults. They must help prepare these young people for working life and for their entry into employment by offering them numerous opportunities for contact and exchanges with the outside world: work experience, various activities conducted with adults, conferences given by outside speakers, etc.

- Know-how and technology change so rapidly that all adults needs to continue learning throughout their lives, whether for their own personal needs or those of their job. Schools, at least these new types of school, are places for all age groups.

- Information technologies, which are developing at great speed, mean that distance working will be possible, indeed already is so. There will doubtless be a "relocation" of school work. Pupils or students will, from their own homes, have access to the most diverse and detailed sources of information, whether in their own country or at the other end of the world. Without leaving his desk, in his own home, a student can have the help of a tutor or teacher. In schools themselves, courses can be received which are actually given far away; interactive dialogue is possible, and questions can be put to a lecturer thousands of kilometres away; information networks give access to databanks. This decentralisation of the sources of learning and the possibilities of transmitting information will lead to a new type of organisation of scolarity which is perhaps difficult to guess at accurately today, but the main feature will no doubt be greater interpenetration between what is still called "inside" and the "outside" of the school; it may even lead to this distinction losing any relevance.

Schools are an integral part of the society in which they are situated. Ensuring the protection of premises and the atmosphere of tranquillity required for study does not mean that this fact is denied: a school does not operate in a vacuum but exists here and now in a given society whose problems it cannot ignore, problems whose good and bad aspects of which will affect it, whether it wishes or not.

If the social climate deteriorates and families in distress are no longer able to bring up their children properly, the negative effects will be felt immediately at school. Social activities organised at school are not something foreign to its vocation but a useful, and sometimes indispensable, contribution to a wider task which incorporates its own narrower one. Thus, in severely disadvantaged neighbourhoods, it is impossible to teach the children until the parents themselves have been educated. More generally, it is clear that involving parents, grandparents and all the adults of a neighbourhood or village has a beneficial effect on the work of the children at school. As Jean-Louis Derouet said, "what the school is being asked to do is to open up to a new mission, to be concerned about the community environment in which it operates".

However, schools must not allow themselves to be taken over or overwhelmed by the problems of their environment. They should not have a passive attitude towards external demands or pressures. They must, on the contrary, adopt a results-oriented approach, take initiatives and formulate a teaching plan. The move towards openness must come from the inside. "Education is part of society. If society becomes more open to new ideas, education and the use of school buildings must reflect this openness both psychologically and physically."

Lastly, when the uses of educational buildings are broadened in conditions which respect the vocation and identity of the school, this process is enriching for both the pupils and the staff. As has often been stressed, the economic objective of increasing the return from educational investment and the social objective of ensuring that a school helps satisfy the educational, cultural and social needs of the local community, are not only compatible but legitimate. The result of this dual economic and social approach is not to divert schools from their vocation, to drag them into the outside world and empty them of their substance. On the contrary, by means of the contacts and exchanges to which it gives rise, it broadens the horizons of teachers and the educational experience of pupils. The presence of adults in a school promotes a new atmosphere and enhances the quality of education. It is not the vocation of schools to turn children into walking encyclopaedias or model pupils but to enable them to become autonomous and responsible adults capable of tackling the problems and difficulties of the real world. Schools with a siege mentality cannot do this, but schools with an outward vision, capable of opening up their gates and venturing forth to meet others, can.

Conclusion

School premises which are not sufficiently occupied or used provoke covetous looks, and this is normal in a period of recession when funds are diminishing as needs are increasing. The desire to make, if not full, at least better, use of school premises and equipment is legitimate and accepted by all. However, this objective and the possible ways of achieving it can take many forms. The most common solutions include putting to other uses (shops, housing) some of the premises insufficiently occupied due to a fall in enrolment; lending or renting out equipment when the pupils are not in school – during the holidays, at weekends or in the evenings; or sharing the use of certain facilities during the day. They require practical measures of an architectural, organisational or managerial nature but have relatively little impact on school actors: teachers and pupils do no meet other users in the case of alternative uses. When facilities are shared, the primary objective is to ensure good relations between the different groups.

But a school is not made up of its premises alone. It is also, and above all, a centre of resources: the teachers working there and the equipment installed constitute a considerable pool of resources in the documentary, scientific, technological and artistic field, amongst others, which are often unique in a neighbourhood or village. A school does not only offer a given number of square metres or possibilities for accommodation or catering, it also represents a wealth of potential for training and cultural events.

To think of broadening the use of educational buildings solely in terms of a quest for increased profits from the space available would be simplistic. Thus, the objective of most of the approaches presented and analysed at the seminar was to make full use of schools, involving **both their premises and their expertise** in the fields of education, technology and culture, which amounts to envisaging an extension and opening-up of the school's very vocation. Schools thus become centres of activities and recreation for young people, places for training adults, centres for the spread of technology to small and medium-sized businesses, and educational and cultural centres for the whole community.

But is there not a risk in this movement towards expansion, that the school as such will disappear, diluted within a wider policy englobing the answer to all of society's social needs? Does the specific function of instructing and educating children of "school age" not need to be emphasized and preserved? Opening up to the "social demand" of a rapidly changing society is both inevitable and a source of enrichment for children. But schools cannot be made subordinate to local needs alone. As Jean-Louis Derouet said, "Goals of equality of opportunity, social and geographic mobility and access to universal values are also part of the missions of schools". A "new equilibrium" has yet to be found in which the quest for improved use of school buildings can be reconciled with the need to open up to the outside and the necessary respect for the identity of the school.

References

Copies of these unpublished papers, presented at the PEB seminar held in Lyon,
France in 1995, may be obtained by writing to:
PEB Secretariat, OECD, 2 rue André-Pascal, 75775 PARIS Cedex 16, France.

Jean-Louis Derouet, *Opening up the school: some reflections on the French experience.*

Luc Desgagnés, *Broadening the uses of school buildings in Quebec.*

Michael Hacker, *Two decades of school and community collaboration in the United Kingdom.*

André Lafond, *Background report.*

Jan Rocksén and Hans Nolander, *The development of the school system in Örnsköldsvik, Sweden.*

H. James Schroeer, *Full-service schools: a Florida perspective.*

Harriet Sinnige, *Broadening the use of educational buildings: Dutch experiences.*

Roy Sowden, *The Dukeries Complex: a place for the family.*

Kelvin Trimper, *Golden Grove Secondary Education Complex, South Australia.*

MAIN SALES OUTLETS OF OECD PUBLICATIONS
PRINCIPAUX POINTS DE VENTE DES PUBLICATIONS DE L'OCDE

ARGENTINA – ARGENTINE
Carlos Hirsch S.R.L.
Galería Güemes, Florida 165, 4° Piso
1333 Buenos Aires   Tel. (1) 331.1787 y 331.2391
Telefax: (1) 331.1787

AUSTRALIA – AUSTRALIE
D.A. Information Services
648 Whitehorse Road, P.O.B 163
Mitcham, Victoria 3132   Tel. (03) 9210.7777
Telefax: (03) 9210.7788

AUSTRIA – AUTRICHE
Gerold & Co.
Graben 31
Wien I   Tel. (0222) 533.50.14
Telefax: (0222) 512.47.31.29

BELGIUM – BELGIQUE
Jean De Lannoy
Avenue du Roi 202 Koningslaan
B-1060 Bruxelles   Tel. (02) 538.51.69/538.08.41
Telefax: (02) 538.08.41

CANADA
Renouf Publishing Company Ltd.
1294 Algoma Road
Ottawa, ON K1B 3W8   Tel. (613) 741.4333
Telefax: (613) 741.5439
Stores:
61 Sparks Street
Ottawa, ON K1P 5R1   Tel. (613) 238.8985
12 Adelaide Street West
Toronto, ON M5H 1L6   Tel. (416) 363.3171
Telefax: (416)363.59.63

Les Éditions La Liberté Inc.
3020 Chemin Sainte-Foy
Sainte-Foy, PQ G1X 3V6   Tel. (418) 658.3763
Telefax: (418) 658.3763

Federal Publications Inc.
165 University Avenue, Suite 701
Toronto, ON M5H 3B8   Tel. (416) 860.1611
Telefax: (416) 860.1608

Les Publications Fédérales
1185 Université
Montréal, QC H3B 3A7   Tel. (514) 954.1633
Telefax: (514) 954.1635

CHINA – CHINE
China National Publications Import
Export Corporation (CNPIEC)
16 Gongti E. Road, Chaoyang District
P.O. Box 88 or 50
Beijing 100704 PR   Tel. (01) 506.6688
Telefax: (01) 506.3101

CHINESE TAIPEI – TAIPEI CHINOIS
Good Faith Worldwide Int'l. Co. Ltd.
9th Floor, No. 118, Sec. 2
Chung Hsiao E. Road
Taipei   Tel. (02) 391.7396/391.7397
Telefax: (02) 394.9176

**CZECH REPUBLIC –
RÉPUBLIQUE TCHÈQUE**
Artia Pegas Press Ltd.
Narodni Trida 25
POB 825
111 21 Praha 1   Tel. (2) 242 246 04
Telefax: (2) 242 278 72

DENMARK – DANEMARK
Munksgaard Book and Subscription Service
35, Nørre Søgade, P.O. Box 2148
DK-1016 København K   Tel. (33) 12.85.70
Telefax: (33) 12.93.87

EGYPT – ÉGYPTE
Middle East Observer
41 Sherif Street
Cairo   Tel. 392.6919
Telefax: 360-6804

FINLAND – FINLANDE
Akateeminen Kirjakauppa
Keskuskatu 1, P.O. Box 128
00100 Helsinki
Subscription Services/Agence d'abonnements :
P.O. Box 23
00371 Helsinki   Tel. (358 0) 121 4416
Telefax: (358 0) 121.4450

FRANCE
OECD/OCDE
Mail Orders/Commandes par correspondance :
2, rue André-Pascal
75775 Paris Cedex 16   Tel. (33-1) 45.24.82.00
Telefax: (33-1) 49.10.42.76
Telex: 640048 OCDE
Internet: Compte.PUBSINQ @ oecd.org
Orders via Minitel, France only/
Commandes par Minitel, France exclusivement :
36 15 OCDE
OECD Bookshop/Librairie de l'OCDE :
33, rue Octave-Feuillet
75016 Paris   Tel. (33-1) 45.24.81.81
(33-1) 45.24.81.67
Dawson
B.P. 40
91121 Palaiseau Cedex   Tel. 69.10.47.00
Telefax: 64.54.83.26

Documentation Française
29, quai Voltaire
75007 Paris   Tel. 40.15.70.00
Economica
49, rue Héricart
75015 Paris   Tel. 45.78.12.92
Telefax: 40.58.15.70
Gibert Jeune (Droit-Économie)
6, place Saint-Michel
75006 Paris   Tel. 43.25.91.19
Librairie du Commerce International
10, avenue d'Iéna
75016 Paris   Tel. 40.73.34.60
Librairie Dunod
Université Paris-Dauphine
Place du Maréchal-de-Lattre-de-Tassigny
75016 Paris   Tel. 44.05.40.13
Librairie Lavoisier
11, rue Lavoisier
75008 Paris   Tel. 42.65.39.95
Librairie des Sciences Politiques
30, rue Saint-Guillaume
75007 Paris   Tel. 45.48.36.02
P.U.F.
49, boulevard Saint-Michel
75005 Paris   Tel. 43.25.83.40
Librairie de l'Université
12a, rue Nazareth
13100 Aix-en-Provence   Tel. (16) 42.26.18.08
Documentation Française
165, rue Garibaldi
69003 Lyon   Tel. (16) 78.63.32.23
Librairie Decitre
29, place Bellecour
69002 Lyon   Tel. (16) 72.40.54.54
Librairie Sauramps
Le Triangle
34967 Montpellier Cedex 2 Tel. (16) 67.58.85.15
Telefax: (16) 67.58.27.36

A la Sorbonne Actual
23, rue de l'Hôtel-des-Postes
06000 Nice   Tel. (16) 93.13.77.75
Telefax: (16) 93.80.75.69

GERMANY – ALLEMAGNE
OECD Publications and Information Centre
August-Bebel-Allee 6
D-53175 Bonn   Tel. (0228) 959.120
Telefax: (0228) 959.12.17

GREECE – GRÈCE
Librairie Kauffmann
Mavrokordatou 9
106 78 Athens   Tel. (01) 32.55.321
Telefax: (01) 32.30.320

HONG-KONG
Swindon Book Co. Ltd.
Astoria Bldg. 3F
34 Ashley Road, Tsimshatsui
Kowloon, Hong Kong   Tel. 2376.2062
Telefax: 2376.0685

HUNGARY – HONGRIE
Euro Info Service
Margitsziget, Európa Ház
1138 Budapest   Tel. (1) 111.62.16
Telefax: (1) 111.60.61

ICELAND – ISLANDE
Mál Mog Menning
Laugavegi 18, Pósthólf 392
121 Reykjavik   Tel. (1) 552.4240
Telefax: (1) 562.3523

INDIA – INDE
Oxford Book and Stationery Co.
Scindia House
New Delhi 110001   Tel. (11) 331.5896/5308
Telefax: (11) 332.5993
17 Park Street
Calcutta 700016   Tel. 240832

INDONESIA – INDONÉSIE
Pdii-Lipi
P.O. Box 4298
Jakarta 12042   Tel. (21) 573.34.67
Telefax: (21) 573.34.67

IRELAND – IRLANDE
Government Supplies Agency
Publications Section
4/5 Harcourt Road
Dublin 2   Tel. 661.31.11
Telefax: 475.27.60

ISRAEL – ISRAËL
Praedicta
5 Shatner Street
P.O. Box 34030
Jerusalem 91430   Tel. (2) 52.84.90/1/2
Telefax: (2) 52.84.93
R.O.Y. International
P.O. Box 13056
Tel Aviv 61130   Tel. (3) 546 1423
Telefax: (3) 546 1442
Palestinian Authority/Middle East:
INDEX Information Services
P.O.B. 19502
Jerusalem   Tel. (2) 27.12.19
Telefax: (2) 27.16.34

ITALY – ITALIE
Libreria Commissionaria Sansoni
Via Duca di Calabria 1/1
50125 Firenze   Tel. (055) 64.54.15
Telefax: (055) 64.12.57
Via Bartolini 29
20155 Milano   Tel. (02) 36.50.83

Editrice e Libreria Herder
Piazza Montecitorio 120
00186 Roma   Tel. 679.46.28
     Telefax: 678.47.51

Libreria Hoepli
Via Hoepli 5
20121 Milano   Tel. (02) 86.54.46
     Telefax: (02) 805.28.86

Libreria Scientifica
Dott. Lucio de Biasio 'Aeiou'
Via Coronelli, 6
20146 Milano   Tel. (02) 48.95.45.52
     Telefax: (02) 48.95.45.48

JAPAN – JAPON
OECD Publications and Information Centre
Landic Akasaka Building
2-3-4 Akasaka, Minato-ku
Tokyo 107   Tel. (81.3) 3586.2016
     Telefax: (81.3) 3584.7929

KOREA – CORÉE
Kyobo Book Centre Co. Ltd.
P.O. Box 1658, Kwang Hwa Moon
Seoul   Tel. 730.78.91
     Telefax: 735.00.30

MALAYSIA – MALAISIE
University of Malaya Bookshop
University of Malaya
P.O. Box 1127, Jalan Pantai Baru
59700 Kuala Lumpur
Malaysia   Tel. 756.5000/756.5425
     Telefax: 756.3246

MEXICO – MEXIQUE
OECD Publications and Information Centre
Edificio INFOTEC
Av. San Fernando no. 37
Col. Toriello Guerra
Tlalpan C.P. 14050
Mexico D.F.
     Tel. (525) 606 00 11 Extension 100
     Fax: (525) 606 13 07

Revistas y Periodicos Internacionales S.A. de C.V.
Florencia 57 - 1004
Mexico, D.F. 06600   Tel. 207.81.00
     Telefax: 208.39.79

NETHERLANDS – PAYS-BAS
SDU Uitgeverij Plantijnstraat
Externe Fondsen
Postbus 20014
2500 EA's-Gravenhage   Tel. (070) 37.89.880
Voor bestellingen: Telefax: (070) 34.75.778

**NEW ZEALAND –
NOUVELLE-ZÉLANDE**
GPLegislation Services
P.O. Box 12418
Thorndon, Wellington   Tel. (04) 496.5655
     Telefax: (04) 496.5698

NORWAY – NORVÈGE
NIC INFO A/S
Bertrand Narvesens vei 2
P.O. Box 6512 Etterstad
0606 Oslo 6   Tel. (022) 57.33.00
     Telefax: (022) 68.19.01

PAKISTAN
Mirza Book Agency
65 Shahrah Quaid-E-Azam
Lahore 54000   Tel. (42) 353.601
     Telefax: (42) 231.730

PHILIPPINE – PHILIPPINES
International Booksource Center Inc.
Rm 179/920 Cityland 10 Condo Tower 2
HV dela Costa Ext cor Valero St.
Makati Metro Manila   Tel. (632) 817 9676
     Telefax: (632) 817 1741

POLAND – POLOGNE
Ars Polona
00-950 Warszawa
Krakowskie Przedmieácie 7   Tel. (22) 264760
     Telefax: (22) 268673

PORTUGAL
Livraria Portugal
Rua do Carmo 70-74
Apart. 2681
1200 Lisboa   Tel. (01) 347.49.82/5
     Telefax: (01) 347.02.64

SINGAPORE – SINGAPOUR
Gower Asia Pacific Pte Ltd.
Golden Wheel Building
41, Kallang Pudding Road, No. 04-03
Singapore 1334   Tel. 741.5166
     Telefax: 742.9356

SPAIN – ESPAGNE
Mundi-Prensa Libros S.A.
Castelló 37, Apartado 1223
Madrid 28001   Tel. (91) 431.33.99
     Telefax: (91) 575.39.98

Mundi-Prensa Barcelona
Consell de Cent No. 391
08009 – Barcelona   Tel. (93) 488.34.92
     Telefax: (93) 487.76.59

Llibreria de la Generalitat
Palau Moja
Rambla dels Estudis, 118
08002 – Barcelona
     (Subscripcions) Tel. (93) 318.80.12
     (Publicacions) Tel. (93) 302.67.23
     Telefax: (93) 412.18.54

SRI LANKA
Centre for Policy Research
c/o Colombo Agencies Ltd.
No. 300-304, Galle Road
Colombo 3   Tel. (1) 574240, 573551-2
     Telefax: (1) 575394, 510711

SWEDEN – SUÈDE
CE Fritzes AB
S–106 47 Stockholm   Tel. (08) 690.90.90
     Telefax: (08) 20.50.21

Subscription Agency/Agence d'abonnements :
Wennergren-Williams Info AB
P.O. Box 1305
171 25 Solna   Tel. (08) 705.97.50
     Telefax: (08) 27.00.71

SWITZERLAND – SUISSE
Maditec S.A. (Books and Periodicals - Livres
et périodiques)
Chemin des Palettes 4
Case postale 266
1020 Renens VD 1   Tel. (021) 635.08.65
     Telefax: (021) 635.07.80

Librairie Payot S.A.
4, place Pépinet
CP 3212
1002 Lausanne   Tel. (021) 320.25.11
     Telefax: (021) 320.25.14

Librairie Unilivres
6, rue de Candolle
1205 Genève   Tel. (022) 320.26.23
     Telefax: (022) 329.73.18

Subscription Agency/Agence d'abonnements :
Dynapresse Marketing S.A.
38, avenue Vibert
1227 Carouge   Tel. (022) 308.07.89
     Telefax: (022) 308.07.99

See also – Voir aussi :
OECD Publications and Information Centre
August-Bebel-Allee 6
D-53175 Bonn (Germany)   Tel. (0228) 959.120
     Telefax: (0228) 959.12.17

THAILAND – THAÏLANDE
Suksit Siam Co. Ltd.
113, 115 Fuang Nakhon Rd.
Opp. Wat Rajbopith
Bangkok 10200   Tel. (662) 225.9531/2
     Telefax: (662) 222.5188

TUNISIA – TUNISIE
Grande Librairie Spécialisée
Fendri Ali
Avenue Haffouz Imm El-Intilaka
Bloc B 1 Sfax 3000   Tel. (216-4) 296 855
     Telefax: (216-4) 298.270

TURKEY – TURQUIE
Kültür Yayinlari Is-Türk Ltd. Sti.
Atatürk Bulvari No. 191/Kat 13
Kavaklidere/Ankara
     Tel. (312) 428.11.40 Ext. 2458
     Telefax: (312) 417 24 90
Dolmabahce Cad. No. 29
Besiktas/Istanbul   Tel. (212) 260 7188

UNITED KINGDOM – ROYAUME-UNI
HMSO
Gen. enquiries   Tel. (171) 873 8242
Postal orders only:
P.O. Box 276, London SW8 5DT
Personal Callers HMSO Bookshop
49 High Holborn, London WC1V 6HB
     Telefax: (171) 873 8416
Branches at: Belfast, Birmingham, Bristol,
Edinburgh, Manchester

UNITED STATES – ÉTATS-UNIS
OECD Publications and Information Center
2001 L Street N.W., Suite 650
Washington, D.C. 20036-4922 Tel. (202) 785.6323
     Telefax: (202) 785.0350

Subscriptions to OECD periodicals may also be
placed through main subscription agencies.

Les abonnements aux publications périodiques de
l'OCDE peuvent être souscrits auprès des
principales agences d'abonnement.

Orders and inquiries from countries where Distribu-
tors have not yet been appointed should be sent to:
OECD Publications Service, 2, rue André-Pascal,
75775 Paris Cedex 16, France.

Les commandes provenant de pays où l'OCDE n'a
pas encore désigné de distributeur peuvent être
adressées à : OCDE, Service des Publications,
2, rue André-Pascal, 75775 Paris Cedex 16, France.

1-1996